MW01229599

Copyright © 2023 by Danyell Welsh

All rights reserved. This book or parts thereof may not be reproduced in any form, stored in any retrieval system, or transmitted in any form by any means—electronic, mechanical, photocopy, recording, or otherwise—without prior written permission of the publisher, except as provided by United States of America copyright law.

ISBN 979-8-9887732-0-7

Library of Congress Control Number: 2023914086

Book Cover and Illustrations by Micheala Angelena
Edited by Renita King and Danyell Welsh

Printed in the United States of America.

First Edition, 2023.

# THE ABCs
# FOR
# BOSS BABIES

Written by Danyell Welsh

*To my siblings:*

*Ares, Christina, Jr., and King.*

*Thank you for being my inspiration.*

# This book belongs to:

_____

Illustrated by:
Micheala Angelena

Allow me to introduce Damilola, one of your amiable guides on this journey to financial literacy! Dami is a vibrant fourth grader who lives in Brooklyn. With her perfectly styled Afro Puffs and overflowing piggy bank, Dami is dedicated to teaching her peers all about money!

Meet Lapu,
the adventurous credit
guru of the group. Lapu is
a 10-year-old with a
passion for learning new
facts about money.
Join him as he classifies
his tax deductions and
builds his credit score
in the animated world
of this book!

Need a stylish budget spreadsheet to manage your finances? Yara's got you covered! She is the youngest of the guides but is also the most innovative. With Yara as your guide, you'll see that good money management involves setting S.M.A.R.T. goals and making responsible decisions!

Nadav loves to stash his leftover lunch money for rainy days. Each month, he cheerily shares his savings challenges with classmates during assembly. Whether it's explaining the importance of being debt-free or compound interest, Nadav makes learning about money interesting and fun!

# A

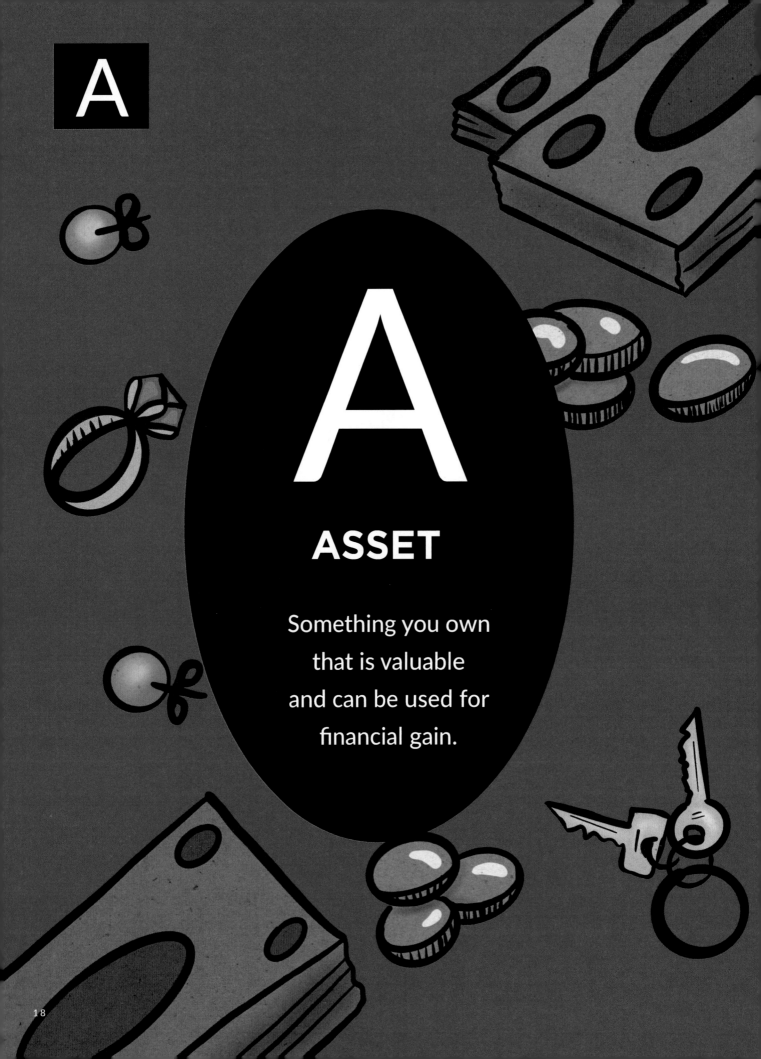

# A

## ASSET

Something you own
that is valuable
and can be used for
financial gain.

# A=L+OE

A (assets) = L (liabilities) + OE (owner's equity)

Assets = Liablities + Owner's Equity

ASSETS = LIABILITIES + OWNER'S EQUITY

B

Income

$ —

$ —

$ —

$ —

Total :—

# B
## BUDGET

A personalized money plan that helps you track your spending.

Expenses

$ ____

$ ____

$ ____

$ ____

$ ____

$ ____

otal:

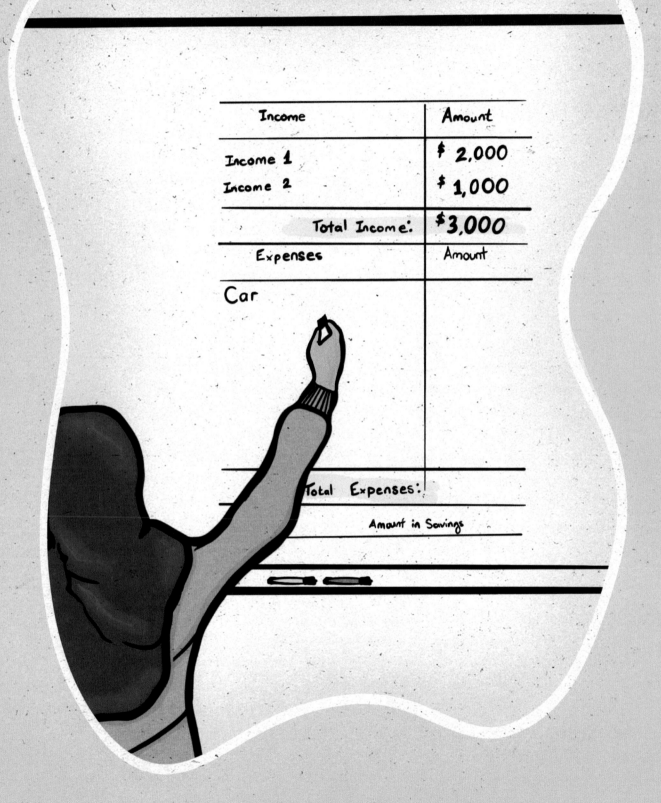

| Income | Amount |
|---|---|
| Income 1 | $ 2,000 |
| Income 2 | $ 1,000 |
| Total Income: | $3,000 |
| Expenses | Amount |
| Car | |
| | |
| Total Expenses: | |
| Amount in Savings | |

**C**

# C

## CREDIT

Money you borrow
to buy things now
with the promise to
pay back later.

# You can check your own credit for free and it does NOT hurt your score.

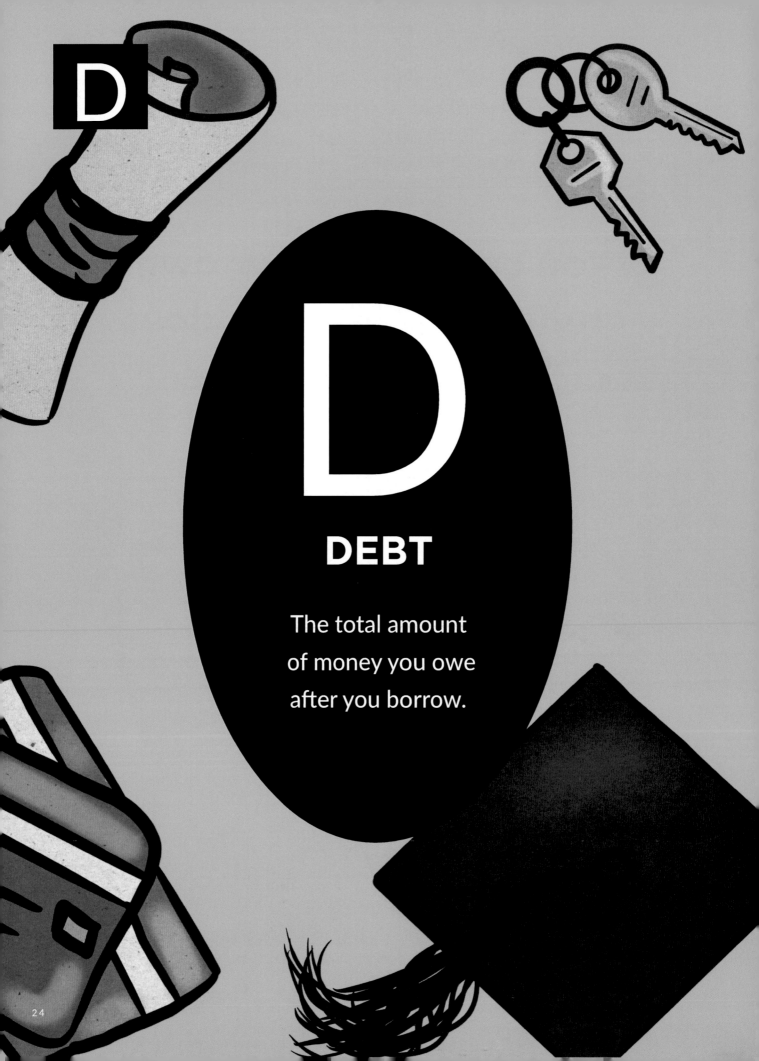

# D

## DEBT

The total amount
of money you owe
after you borrow.

# E

## EXPENSES

The money needed
to pay for the cost of
activities, resources,
and services.

# What are some examples of expenses?

_____

_____

_____

_____

# F

# F

## FICO SCORE

An important type of credit score used to determine your buying power.

# Fico Score Factors

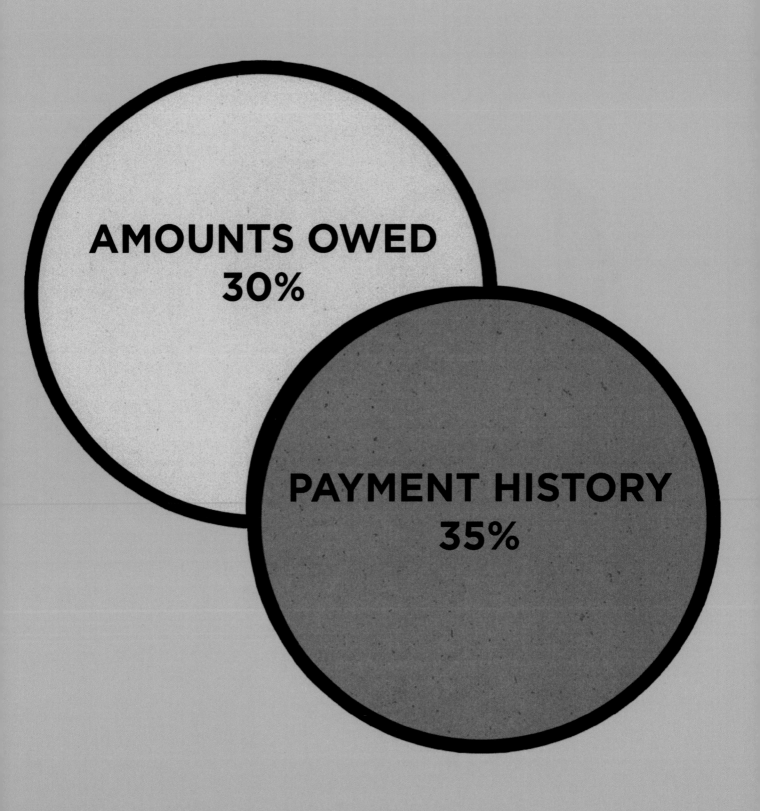

# Your FICO score typically ranges from 300 to 850

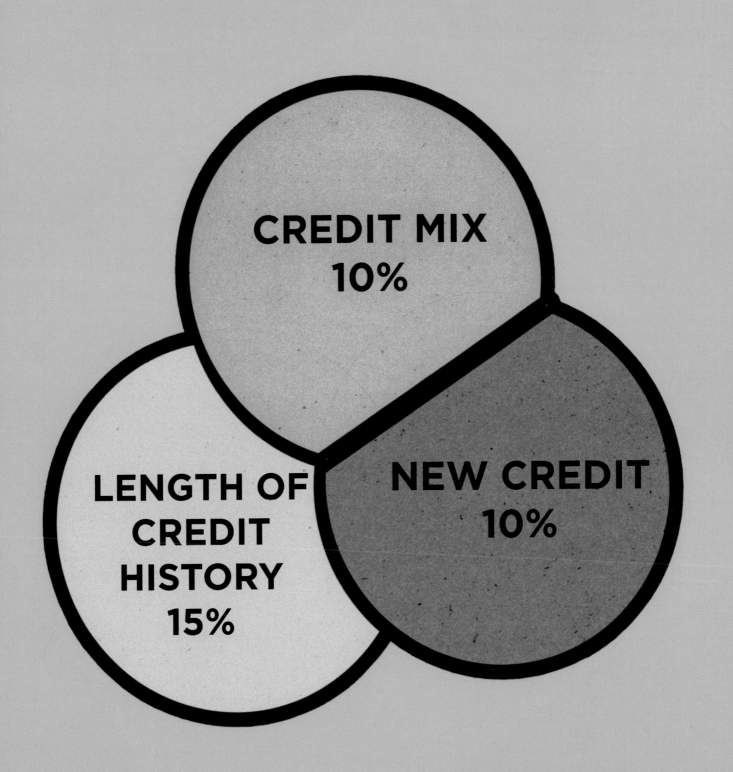

# G

## GROSS INCOME

The total amount
of money you make
BEFORE taxes
and deductions.

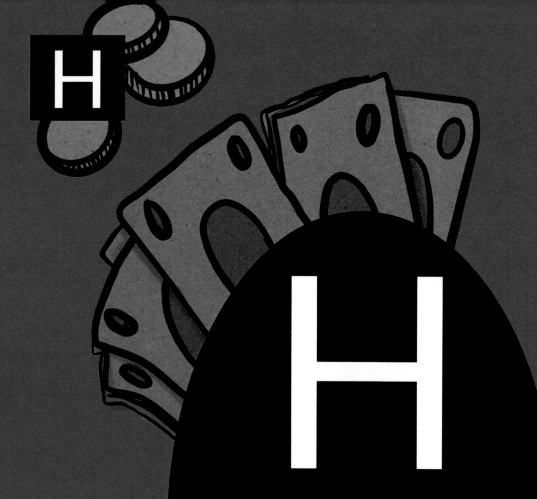

# H

## HEDGE FUND

An exclusively managed
pool of money from
wealthy investors
used to make risky
investments.

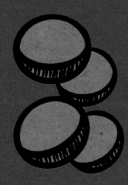

# Hedge Funds

Are riskier than mutual funds

Investors have to meet certain net worth requirements

Often use leverage or "borrowed money" to maximize returns

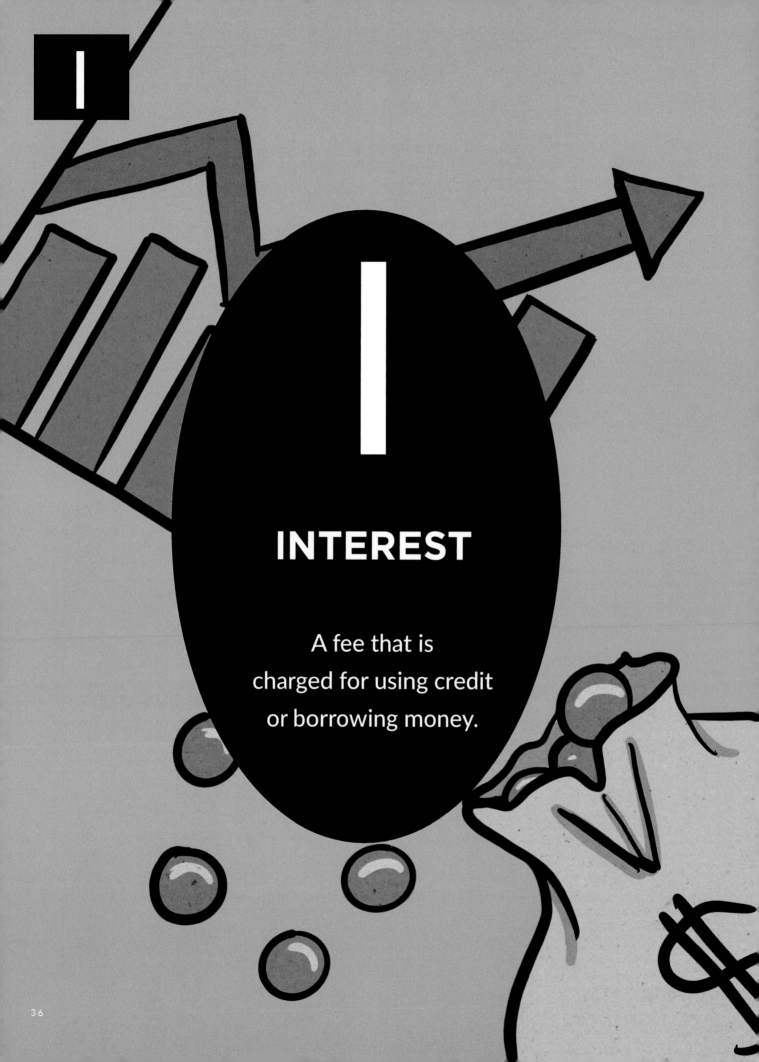

# INTEREST

A fee that is charged for using credit or borrowing money.

# J

## JOINT ACCOUNT

An account that
is equally shared between
two or more people.

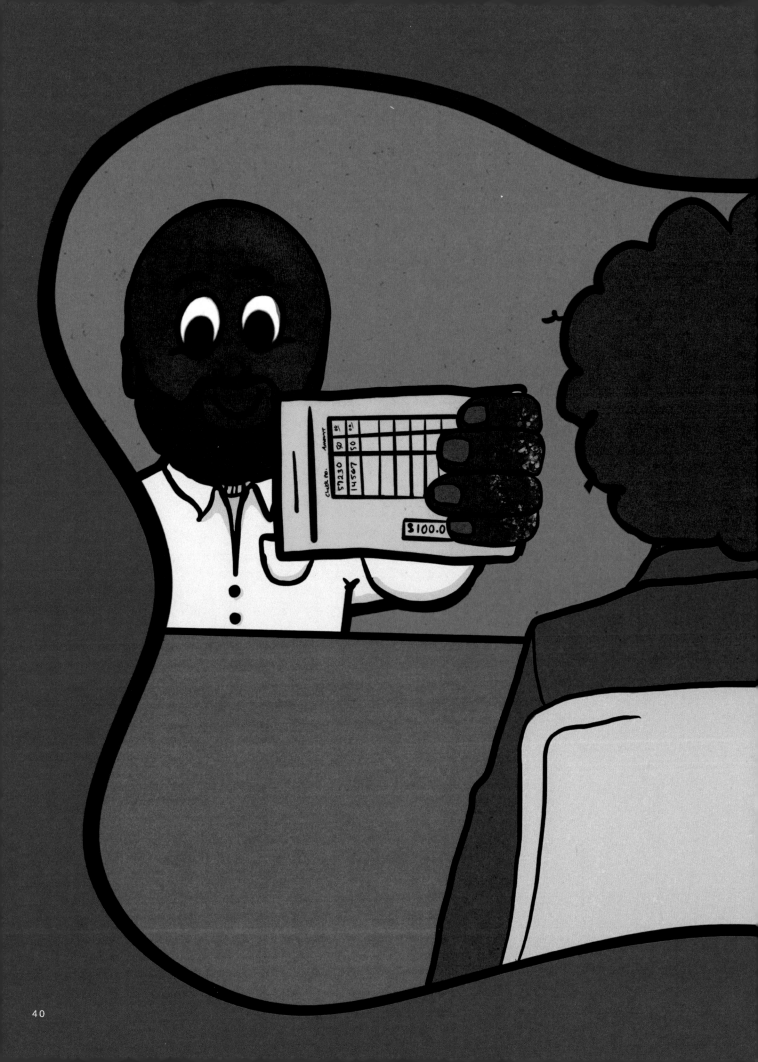

# K

## KEOGH PLAN

A retirement savings plan
for small business owners
and people who
are self-employed.

# L

## LIABILITY

Something that requires
you to spend money
and use resources.

# Liabilities do NOT generate income, they create expenses.

# M

## MUTUAL FUND

A professionally managed, public investment portfolio that uses money from several investors to buy assets.

# Mutual Fund

Invest in a variety of companies and industries

Are less risky and aligned with investment objectives

Are generally more affordable and require lower minimum contributions.

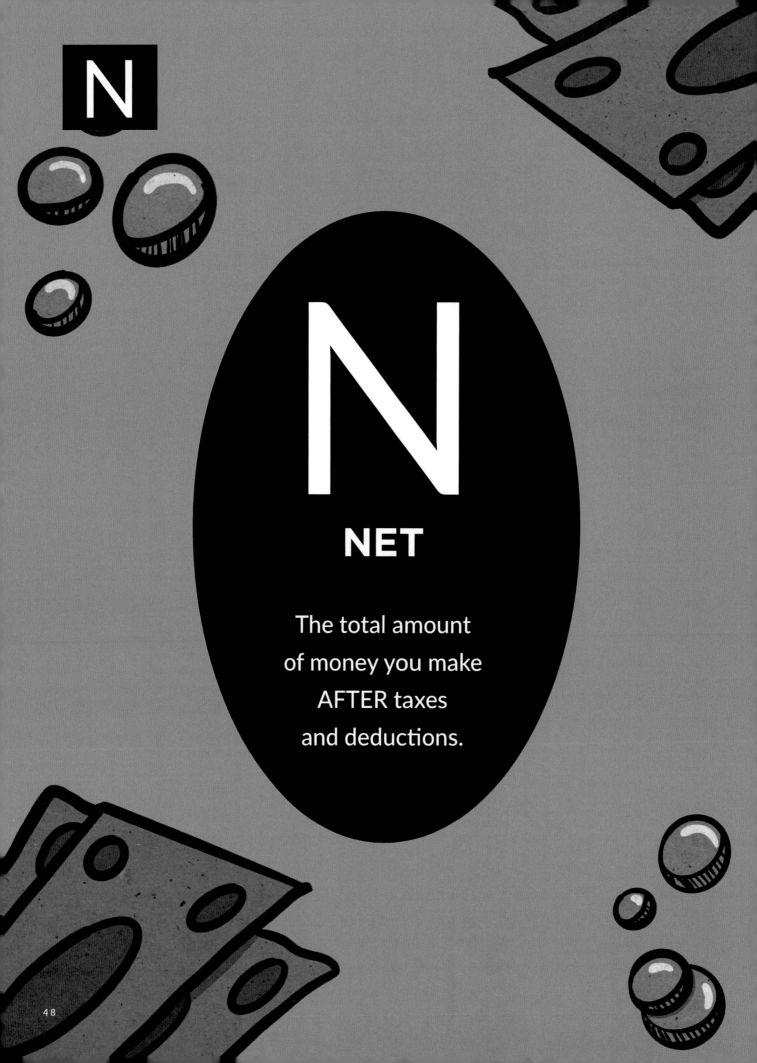

# N

## NET

The total amount
of money you make
AFTER taxes
and deductions.

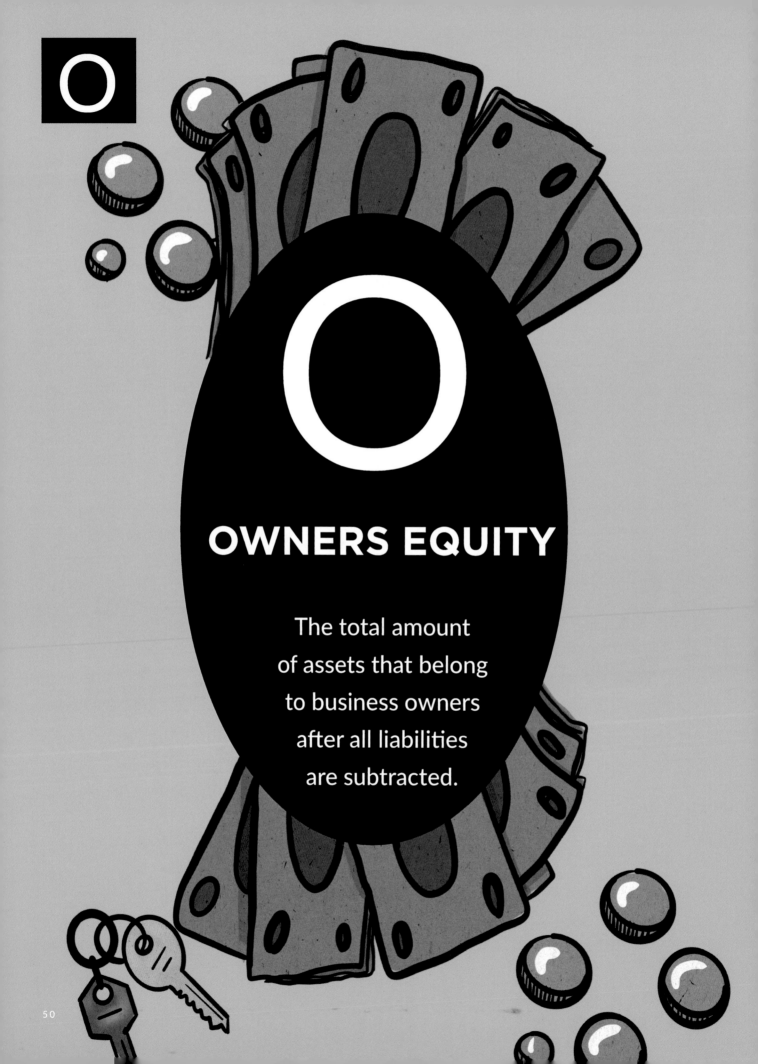

# O

## OWNERS EQUITY

The total amount
of assets that belong
to business owners
after all liabilities
are subtracted.

# OE=A-L

OE (Owner's Equity) = A (assets) - L (liabilities)

Owner's Equity = Assets - Liablities

OWNER'S EQUITY

=

ASSETS

-

LIABILITIES

# P

## P
## PROFIT

The money left after all costs and expenses are paid.

Penny made $75 from selling her Peanut Butter cookies on Tuesday. It cost her $25 for all of the ingredients.

How much profit did she make?

*Use the following equation to solve the problem:*

**Profit = Total Sales - Total Expenses**

_____ = _____ - _____

Q

January

April

July

October

# Q

## QUARTER

Three consecutive months on a financial calendar.

## First Quarter

January

February

March

## Second Quarter

April

May

June

## Third Quarter

July

August

September

## Fourth Quarter

October

November

December

# R

## RESIDUAL PAY

Income earned even after you have completed the work.

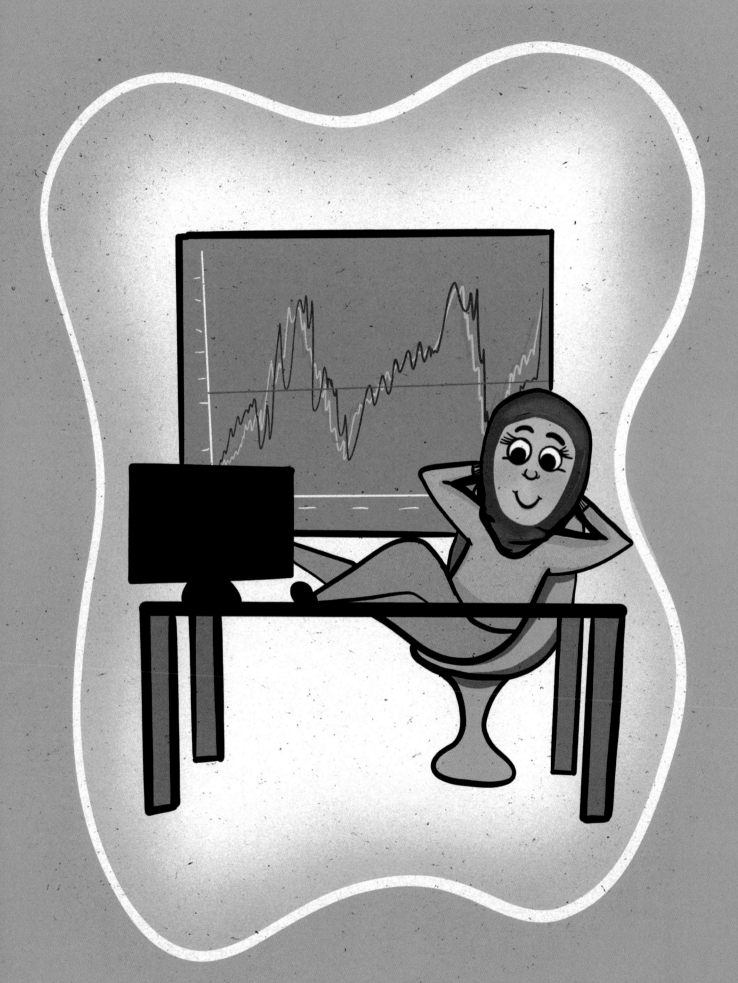

S

# S

## STOCK

Where investors buy
or sell small fractions
of ownership in
public companies.

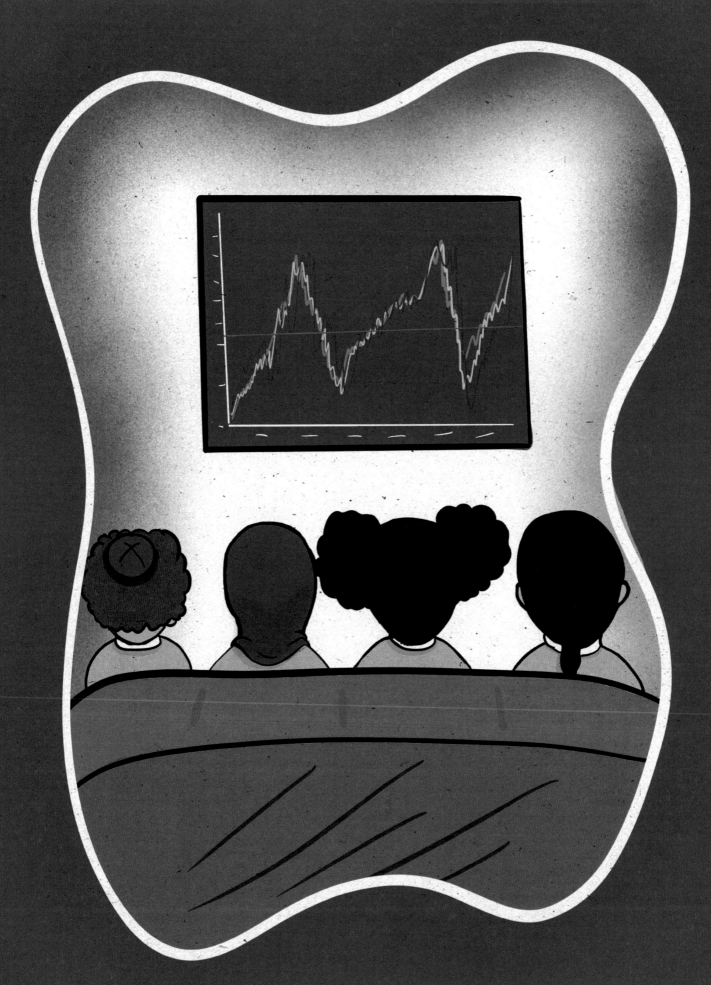

# T

# T

## TAXES

A percentage of money
that must be paid
to the government.

# 9 tax write-offs for business owners

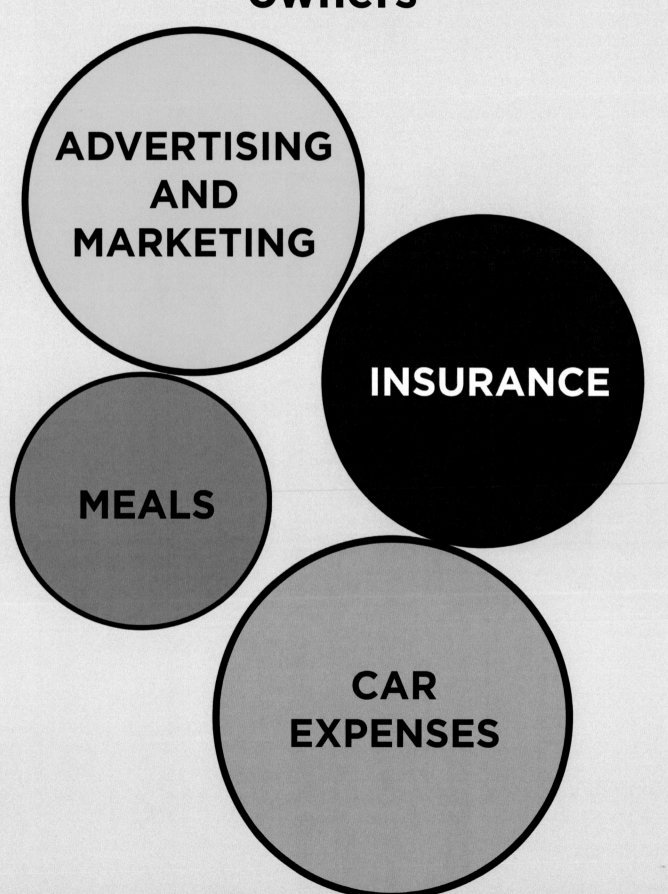

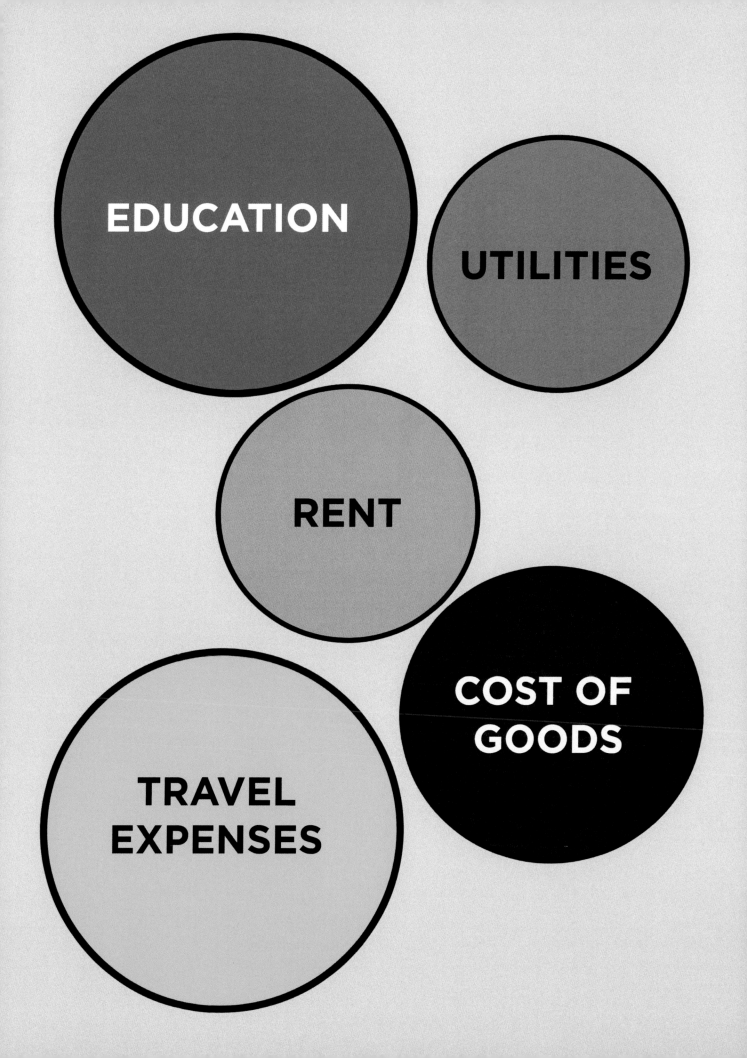

# U

## UTILIZATION

The percentage of
available credit that
you have already used.

# Try to keep your credit card utilization between 20-30%

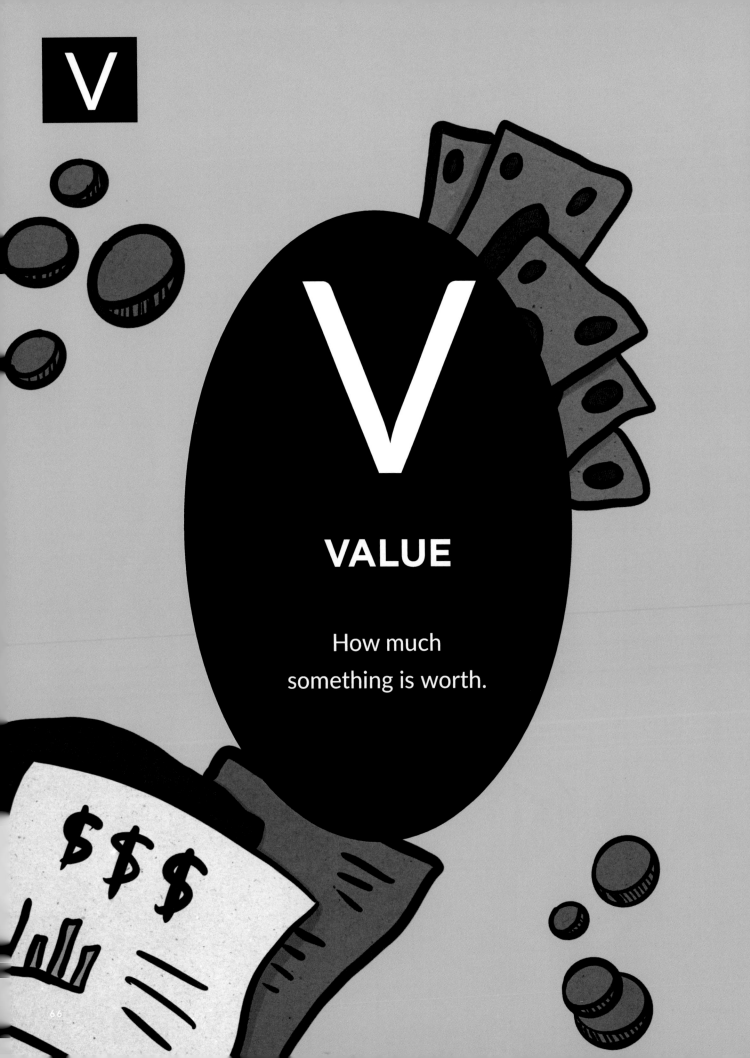

# V

## VALUE

How much
something is worth.

# The value of my shirt is

_____

W

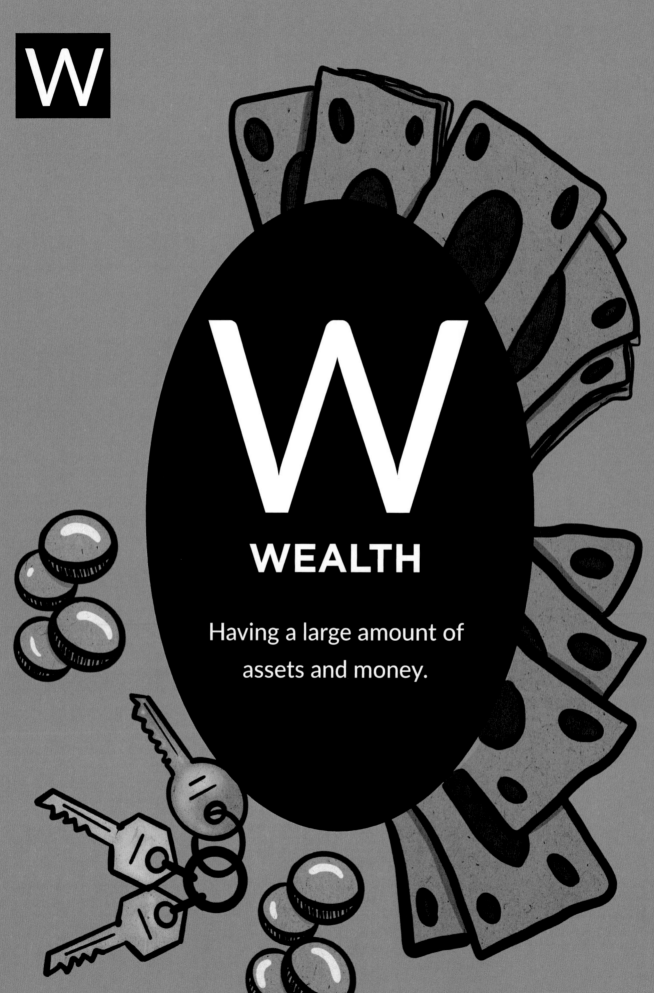

# W

## WEALTH

Having a large amount of
assets and money.

# How else can someone be wealthy?

# X

# XENOCURRENCY

Money used or exchanged
in a country different
from where it was
originally printed.

US DOLLAR

# Y

## YIELD

Income earned from
assets or investments
over a certain period
of time.

# Z

# Z

## ZERO-COUPON BOND

A bond purchased at
a discounted rate
that does not
generate yield until
the bond matures.

# 3 Facts about Z-Bonds

1. **Often come with higher yields than traditional bonds.**

2. **You do NOT receive periodic interest payments.**

3. **Allows investors to earn risk-free interest over a long period.**

Hi! I'm Danyell, a visionary and zealous writer from The East. As the oldest of all my siblings, I developed a keen sense of responsibility for our youth. The ABCs for Boss Babies is my way of giving back while concurrently equipping the community with resources to attain financial literacy.

Made in the USA
Columbia, SC
12 December 2023

964a9d6c-c3fc-41fd-9798-80a3a0f580c0R02